# Settling Your Child in School

## A Parent's Guide

**Michelle Wallis**

Crown House Publishing Limited
www.crownhouse.co.uk

First published in 2003 by
Pascal Press
PO Box 250
Glebe NSW 2037
(02)8585 4044
**www.pascalpress.com.au**
Original ISBN: 1 877085 99 5

Publisher: Vivienne Petris Joannou
Editor: Christine Eslick
Photos by Brand X, Corbis, Eyewire and PhotoDisc


This UK edition published by
Crown House Publishing Ltd
Crown Buildings, Bancyfelin, Carmarthen, Wales, SA33 5ND, UK
**www.crownhouse.co.uk**

and

Crown House Publishing Company LLC
4 Berkeley Street, 1st Floor, Norwalk, CT 06850, USA
**www.CHPUS.com**

**British Library of Cataloguing-in-Publication Data**
A catalogue entry for this book is available from the British Library.

**International Standard Book Number**
**1904424503**

**Library of Congress Control Number**
**2004111448**

Printed and bound in the UK by
*Cromwell Press, Trowbridge, Wiltshire*

# Acknowledgments

For Kristen and Lauren—the best teachers I know!

A special thanks to Anna Gorman, who read and edited this book first; Craig for his love and support; Rachel for keeping my feet on the ground; and my family for always being there.

# Contents

# Introduction

*My decision to write this book came out of my own personal experience of frustration and the lack of information available to me when my daughter began primary school and began to experience a sense of failure. She was, and still is, a terrific girl. She was bright and funny and great with people, but when she started school something happened that changed all that.*

Suddenly, she was no longer the shining star. Suddenly, she was expected to do things at a particular time, in a particular way, and exactly as she was told. Suddenly, she didn't know all the answers, and she would refuse to guess at them for fear of being wrong.

There were a number of things that contributed to my daughter's sense of failure and the on-going struggle she has with her confidence. First, there was the fact that I had no idea she was feeling this way. As a parent, I had assumed she would go to school and learn to read and write and do maths. She would cope just fine because she had gone to preschool and she'd been fine there—there'd been no suggestion that she needed another year at preschool.

Although I hadn't explicitly taught her to read, she knew all about books and loved them just as I do. She wasn't writing when she started school, but she could certainly colour and draw. She knew her ABC—sang it all the time, counted everything and was very social and friendly. I was a school teacher at this time and felt she would do very well at school. She was ready for school, wasn't she?

I have learnt a lot since then. I wanted to see what schools were doing in the areas of reading, writing and arithmetic. As a teacher, I steadily became aware that there was a 'gap' between preschool and the beginning of school. School is different from preschool.

Schools try to prepare parents and children as best they can, and they provide information directly to those who can make it to the familiarisation day, or through brochures and information booklets. Most children do fine, because they are so keen to learn and are eager to please parents, teachers and friends. Some, though, need a little more help to cross that gap, and all can benefit from knowing more rather than less when they start school.

I don't claim to have all the answers, and I cannot guarantee your child's instant success at school. What I have put together is a series of questions, ideas, suggestions and information that I hope you will be able to put to good use to help your child across the gap and into the joy of learning and school.

# 1 Education today

*For many parents, school is a long-distant and best-forgotten memory. Having a child enter the education system today can be quite a shock. A great deal has changed in the way children are educated. No longer do they spend most of their day trapped behind their desk receiving the facts. The focus of education today is to help children become active learners and to develop good thinking skills, not just to get a good number of facts into them.*

Educationalists strive to deliver lessons that are interesting, remove the need for rote learning (learning things by heart by repetition) and engage the child's interest, so that the child is motivated to learn for their own reasons. All this is wonderful—but it can be very confusing for the parent who learnt by rote and only knows that style of education.

## What's different in the classroom?

Enter a primary school classroom today and you will find some things familiar: word lists and spelling charts, numbers, sounds and letters, the alphabet up on the walls and lots of bright colours and interesting posters. The room is supposed to be inviting and interesting for all who enter—that's what teachers strive for in their presentation, and this hasn't changed too much from when you started school.

What the children are doing is quite a bit different though. Classrooms can be noisy hives of activity with children working in many different locations in the room, and not always with the direct instruction of the teacher. Learning centres are used to stimulate children to develop their own understandings: children work in co-operative groups, talking about what they are learning and teaching one another. Children with disabilities may be included in the class group too, and this affects the way the classroom is structured.

The teacher will work with one group focused on a particular concept while the other children pursue their own understandings. This can look very disorganised and can be noisy—but it works very well, allowing children to learn at their own pace and also to develop social skills in the process.

## What are learning centres?

Learning centres can be anything from a formal desk arrangement in each of the corners of the room, to a cardboard box or milk crate that can be moved to any location in the room. Learning centres are designed to provide the stimulation and materials for the children to learn a particular concept or skill in a certain amount of time. Games, worksheets, cut-and-paste activities, listening posts, library corners, talk and chalk, magnetic numbers and letters, puzzles, almost anything you can imagine that can be managed independently by a child can form the learning centre.

Not all learning in the classroom is done in learning centres but a good number of learning-centre activities are encouraged in classrooms. The idea is that the children develop independence and have the freedom to explore their own ideas about the topic or concept under investigation.

## What about discipline?

There have been dramatic shifts in ideas about discipline. Corporal punishment is no longer acceptable, and just as children are expected to be independent learners, they are expected to be responsible for their own behaviour.

When a child misbehaved, the solution used to be to treat the behaviour and train the child to behave appropriately. The focus was on adjusting the child's behaviour to be acceptable. 'Spare the rod and spoil the child' was the common thinking of some twenty or so years ago.

Then came the realisation that corporal punishment had some nasty side effects, such as beginning a cycle of violence that continued after the child had left school. Damage was done to the self-esteem of the children exposed to corporal punishment, and the effects of this also continued after those children had left school. It became clear that changes needed to be made.

Now, the treatment of misbehaviour focuses on why the child might be misbehaving, not just on adjusting the behaviour. Questions are asked, such as:

- Is the child worried that they can't do the work?
- Is the child distracting our attention so that no one realises the work seems too hard?
- Is the child bored because the work is not challenging enough?
- Is there something else going on for this child—at home, in the playground, in the classroom—that is distracting and upsetting them?

All these questions are asked because educationalists believe that if the child is engaged and challenged enough by the work in class there should be no reason for misbehaviour. Naturally, when a teacher begins asking the family questions about why the child is behaving in a particular way, it can be seen as threatening but the teacher is usually just trying to make sense of the behaviour and help solve the problem behaviour.

Producing work for between twenty-five and thirty children in one class-room, and making the work interesting and challenging to each and every one of them, is a difficult task, and teachers don't always get it right. Most teachers manage to do it most of the time for most of the children in their care, though.

Discipline procedures will vary from school to school, and it would be worth asking for a copy of the particular school's policy when your child begins there, so that you know what to expect if things don't go smoothly for your child.

Corporal punishment, verbal abuse, humiliation and intimidation are not effective ways for children to be disciplined, and most schools should have alternatives for these methods. Children are usually warned about their behaviour, told why it is inappropriate at school and, after a number of warnings, given time to think and reflect on their own behaviour and possibly given time out of the classroom. You may be contacted so that you and the school can work together to resolve the inappropriate behaviour.

# What about self-esteem?

The self-esteem of your child will have a large influence on what they achieve in all facets of life, and particularly at school. It is vital that you ensure that your child understands that achievements at school, while very important, are not the only things that are important in life. Many parents place such value on education that when children do not perform at the top of the grade in all things, they begin to believe they are worthless. The unfortunate thing is that only one can be top of the grade, and this expectation to be the 'best' sets many children up for a sense of failure.

Children must be taught to value their own achievements—regardless of where that achievement places them in terms of their peers. The focus should be on having successes at their own level, rather than in comparison with another child of more or less ability. Children can only achieve their potential, and no amount of pressure can improve this because not everyone can be the best at everything. Encourage, support, challenge and celebrate the successes your child achieves in whichever area they succeed in, but don't make them feel worthless because you have set impossible goals.

- Remind your child every day that you love them regardless of how they perform at school.

- Set realistic goals, encourage and support, but don't pressure your child.

- Remind your child every day that they are good/best at lots of different things, especially if they are having trouble at school.

- Keep a record of the things your child achieves, large and small, at school.

- Focus only on what your child is doing, not on what Johnny-next-door is or can do.

In the chapters 'Learning styles' (page 22) and 'Resilience' (page 27) you will find more information about how to help your child see where their strengths are, how to help them recognise their own learning styles and some information about 'bouncing back' despite setbacks and disappointments.

## What can you do to help?

Things have changed quite a lot. Children are expected to pursue their own understandings: they are no longer expected to be passive and just accept what the teacher presents to them. They are expected to ask questions, to be challenged and to challenge the information given to them, and to check for the relevance or truth of what they are being taught. Children in this environment need to be a lot more independent and actively engaged in their education.

Preschools often run orientation programmes in preparation for beginning school. The children come to visit their school, classroom and teacher late in the year before they begin school. Parents are often invited to join their children for this day. These programmes work extremely well, allowing the child the opportunity to meet and explore the school and its staff with the support and assistance of the preschool teacher and parents.

If your preschool does not have such a programme in place there are a number of things you can do even before your child begins school:

- Drive by the school frequently and tell your child that it is their school.
- Build excitement by talking about all the fun things your child will get to do at school.
- Hide your own anxiety because the child will sense it and become anxious too.
- Visit the school and walk around the grounds with your child, pointing

out classrooms, toilets, office, staffroom, library. (Do this at the end of the day when children are leaving school to give your child a sense of how busy school is. It will also be less conspicuous and you won't interrupt the school day for students and teachers. Schools tend to be a bit suspicious of people lurking in school grounds during the day for safety reasons.)

- Use the toilets at school while you are there. Check your child can lock and unlock doors and manage the taps.

- Find out which will be your child's classroom and visit the room. Looking in at the windows is a beginning; walk in if you can (after school).

- Arrange a time to visit your child's teacher and have a conversation with them and your child. (Make an appointment for this—just as you would to visit the doctor—and don't just turn up. Teachers also have many responsibilities and are very busy.)

- Let your child play on the equipment in the playground when you visit.

The following chapters are designed to help you prepare your child for school. There is a checklist at the end of most chapters to help you see where your child is already achieving and where you can continue to develop their skills and abilities. Within the chapters are suggestions as to how to develop the skills or knowledge. There are lists of activities you can do, suggestions for continuing from each step and ideas about what to develop before beginning school and even after your child has begun school.

Education is a life-long process. Don't think that you can afford to stop teaching and learning once your child has begun school. Your active involvement in your child's education is one of the key ingredients for success.

Good luck, and remember to enjoy and celebrate the process as well as the achievements!

# 2 The basics

## Can your child recognize their name in all kinds of scripts?

It is important that your child can recognise their name in all kinds of scripts so that they know whether or not they have their own lunchbox, school jumper, book and schoolwork. It will help your child's esteem as well to be able to write their own name on their work.

- Write your child's name and explain that this says their name.

- Write your child's name and then have them trace over it. Do it often enough so that they come to recognise the letters in their name.

- Build to dotted writing: your child joins the dots to ultimately write their own name.

- Print the child's name on the computer in a variety of scripts to ensure that they know what it looks like. This teaches your child to recognise that the letters hold the same value even when the writing is different.

- Ensure that your child's name is written with a capital letter at the beginning and lower case for the rest (e.g. 'Kristen' not 'KRISTEN'). Prevent bad habits forming right from the beginning.

## Does your child know the basics?

Make sure your child knows these:

- their address

- their phone number

- parents' names

- their date of birth

- name of their school
- name of their teacher.

These are things that the child will need to know for their whole school life, and they can be helpful if the child ever gets lost. Knowing these things will make your child proud in those first few weeks.

## Can your child dress/undress without help?

School uniforms tend to be child-friendly tracksuits and T-shirts so that children can get in and out of them easily. It will be important that your child can dress and undress without help for school swimming programmes, drama, dress-ups and sports activities.

Have your child practise:

- dressing and undressing as part of dress-up activities
- dressing and undressing themselves when they get up and when they go to bed at night
- doing up buttons, zips and shoe laces.

# Can your child do up shoes?

It is no longer necessary for children to struggle with shoe laces if they can't manage them when they begin school. Most school shoe suppliers have sensibly begun to offer a range of shoes to suit all types of children.

Most schools will insist on shoes rather than runners or trainers because they are more supportive of little feet. School shoes are sturdier and less likely to absorb rain, they are also usually made with tougher materials and children are less likely to suffer a needle-stick injury through school shoes.

Consider these alternatives for lace-up shoes:

- shoes with Velcro fastenings
- shoes with buckles
- slip-on shoes.

# Does your child have a lunchbox?

It is important at school that children know their own property. Having a lunchbox that your child recognises will save some hassle at school, especially when the children become involved in shared lunches with friends or on excursions, where they eat lunch at a location other than their own classroom. (This won't usually happen in the first term of school.)

Check these:

- Can your child unwrap food in cling film?
- Can your child open plastic pockets and packets of crisps or biscuits?
- Can your child open any plastic containers you might use?

# Does your child eat at regular times during the day?

School can be hard on young tummies, because there is an expectation that food will only be eaten at certain times in the day. If a child is not used to this routine, it can be hard for them to understand and learning can suffer because of a highly distracting grumbling tummy.

- Check school meal times when you visit.
- Have a snack at the same time as morning break each day.
- Lunchtime can be any time between 12.30 and 1.00 pm. Eat lunch at the same time as they do at school before school begins.
- Match any snack breaks they are likely to have.

Breakfast becomes very important once school begins. Ensure your child:

- eats a good filling breakfast before school;
- eats early enough to still get to school on time!

# Does your child know how to use the toilet alone?

Being able to use the toilet alone is obviously important. Children must know about toileting and hygiene before they get to school.

Naturally, school teachers are aware young bladders need training and will usually allow breaks for toileting. Many will take whole classes to the toilets during the day to ensure there are fewer interruptions during lesson times. But if your child does have to go to the toilet during lessons it means that not only is your child's learning interrupted but that of other children as well.

- Have your child use the toilet at regular intervals, and close to the time for breaks in the school day.
- Encourage your child to go even when they don't need to at this time.

# Does your child have a regular bedtime?

We all know that getting enough sleep is important to ensure we are performing at our best. It is just as important for young children to have enough sleep at regular times.

Setting a bedtime allows your child the comfort of knowing exactly when they will be in bed. When they begin school and there are so many big changes going on, it is important that some things (especially those at home) remain regular and known. Having a regular bedtime before school begins can help your child feel secure and confident, in addition to being well rested.

- Set a regular bedtime and stick to it!
- Ensure your child is getting enough sleep.
- Get your child up early enough to get to school on time.

# Checklist for the basics

| Is your child ready? | Yes/No |
|---|---|
| Can your child recognise their name in all kinds of scripts? | |
| Does your child know their address? | |
| Does your child know their phone number? | |
| Does your child know your name and your partner's name? | |
| Does your child know the name of their school? | |
| Does your child know the name of their teacher? | |
| Does your child know their birthday? | |
| Can your child dress/undress without help? | |
| Can your child put shoes on and take them off without help? | |
| Does your child have a lunchbox? | |

Can your child unwrap food in cling film?

Can your child open plastic containers?

Can your child unwrap crisps, biscuits and plastic pockets?

Does your child eat at regular times?

Does your child know how to use the toilet and about hygiene?

Does your child use the toilet regularly at 'school' times?

Is your child eating a filling breakfast?

Is your child eating breakfast with enough time to get to school?

Does your child have a regular bedtime?

Is your child getting up in time to get to school?

If you answered no to any of these questions, perhaps you need to refer back to the information in this chapter and begin practising some of the suggestions made there.

# 3  Gross motor skills

## What are gross motor skills?

Gross motor skills are all the broad and large movements we are able to perform. As babies, we have little or no control of our bodies, and we gradually develop motor control (control of our muscles). First, we are able to perform very broad movements like swinging an arm in the direction we want to, and then we work up to a level where we can pick up a tiny button from the floor and put it on to a pile of buttons without knocking them over.

Your child should practise large movements to get ready for finer movements later. These gross motor activities will increase muscle tone and motor control.

Make sure your child gets plenty of practice at:

- running
- jumping
- crawling
- catching
- kicking
- throwing
- tipping
- rolling
- hopping
- waving
- clapping
- skipping
- climbing
- swinging

- balancing

- spinning

- pouring

- carrying.

The list of suitable activities is endless, and the good news is that they are all things children usually do naturally while they play.

## Play is never pointless

Play is always the way children develop their skills, experiment with their bodies and develop experience and skills in using their bodies. It is very

important that your child continues to develop and enjoy their physical abilities as much as their intellectual and computer skills. By using their bodies children learn to control the muscles and joints, they build strength and muscle tone that are important for developing the finer motor skills required for such tasks as writing, colouring, drawing and doing up buttons, shoelaces and zippers. Play with your child!

Use big soft balls for:

- throwing

- catching

- rolling on

- swimming with

- rolling to and fro.

Ropes tied in trees are great for swinging from and climbing.

Parks are great because they contain:

- climbing equipment
- ropes
- wooden structures
- monkey bars
- slides
- swings.

These activities all help to build hand strength and co-ordination.

# Using both sides of the body and brain

The co-ordination of using one arm/leg and then the other engages both sides of the brain and gets the messages working between the two sides of the brain. This stimulates nerves and brings about quicker and more fluent communication between the two 'brains', assisting the ability to learn later in life.

Your child will increase co-ordination and reflexes by practising using both sides of the body. Of particular benefit are activities that require the use of both sides of the body one after the other, such as:

- skipping (without a rope)
- swimming
- crawling (crawling up hills and over furniture will add more of a challenge and increase muscle tone)

- climbing in trees, monkey bars or adventure gyms
- running.

This list is not exhaustive but will give you some ideas.

# Checklist for gross motor skills

| Does your child ... | Yes/No |
| --- | --- |
| Run regularly? | |
| Engage in physical games, including jumping, hopping, skipping, running, rolling, climbing, balancing, clapping and waving? | |
| Engage in games with large, soft balls? | |
| Engage in games that include swinging from ropes, climbing up ropes and ladders, using monkey bars, swings and slides? | |
| Swim regularly? | |
| Visit the park regularly? | |

It is very important that your child be active, not just for their physical health but also for the development of the nervous system, including the brain. Physical play helps to create co-ordination, muscle tone and motor control but it is also vitally important in stimulating the brain and all the nerves so that messages are passed quickly and easily between body and brain, and from one side of the brain to the other.

# 4 Fine motor skills and hand–eye co-ordination

## What are fine motor skills?

As motor control becomes better, children are able to do much finer and more dexterous movements. Hand–eye co-ordination is the ability to see that something needs doing and have the hand automatically and without faltering follow through. Ball sports, computer games, video games, writing and many other activities require the co-ordination of seeing and doing in this way.

## Why are they important?

Developing fine motor skills and hand–eye co-ordination is very important for your child's success at school. These skills are essential for writing and many of the other tasks your child will need to perform as part of the school day.

## Preschool and beyond

On the following pages is a list of play activities that will help develop a child's fine motor and hand–eye co-ordination skills. You will notice that many of the activities listed are familiar if your child has attended preschool. Preschool has begun the important work of developing fine motor skills and hand–eye co-ordination. It is important that children have the opportunity to continue these kinds of activities outside the preschool environment.

Try to encourage your child to participate in a few of these activities every day—your child may need your help with some of these games and may be keener to play some of them if you play too!

## Fine motor and hand–eye co-ordination tasks

- colouring pictures from a colouring book

- copying letters, patterns and numbers that you draw

- moulding clay, plasticine or play dough into a ball, snake or various shapes

- punching holes with a hole punch (random or a set design)

- screwing and unscrewing nuts and bolts

- picking up small objects one at a time (e.g. buttons, beads, paperclips, pebbles, gravel, rice grains)

- using clothes pegs to make a chain of clothes pegs

- hand-wringing clothes (helping with the washing)

- using sand, rice or beans for play such as pasting them on to paper

- stacking objects into piles

- using locks and keys

- dressing and undressing self, dolls or teddies

- making chains out of paperclips

- playing 'two cups and a ball', passing the ball from cup to cup without touching it with their hands

- threading macaroni, cotton reels or beads

- playing marbles

- playing with building blocks, Lego and Meccano

- doing jigsaw puzzles

- turning pages when reading a book

- making paper planes and boats
- knitting (using big needles and thick wool)
- screwing tops on to bottles of different sizes
- cooking (e.g. making pastry with their hands and rolling it out or stirring the cooking mixture with a spoon)
- using an egg beater (with water or for real cooking)
- playing 'a handful of objects': picking up as many objects (e.g. beads, macaroni, buttons) as possible with one hand, counting them one by one and seeing if the counting improves
- doing finger painting
- passing a tennis ball or beanbag from one hand to the other or from person to person as quickly as possible
- hitting balloons and keeping them up in the air
- throwing beanbags or large balls at a target (stationary or moving)
- blowing bubbles and catching them with their fingers
- putting on and taking off socks and gloves
- bowling at targets
- hitting a suspended ball (with hand or bat)
- counting small objects (e.g. on an abacus)
- making and playing with a dressing board (zips, press studs, buttons, laces, Velcro and so on)
- tying and untying knots and shoelaces
- playing post box: putting coins, 'letters' and cards into a small box with a slit in the top
- playing with finger puppets and sock puppets
- using a typewriter or computer keyboard
- using a peg board, putting pegs in holes—for older children make this more interesting by getting them to copy a pattern on the board
- using tweezers or tongs to pick up small objects
- weaving and lacing items

- hammering basic woodwork under supervision, using simple tools
- dealing out cards, shuffling cards, making card houses
- dialling telephone numbers
- pouring liquid from one container to a smaller one
- matching coloured pegs to strips of coloured tape around the top of an ice-cream container
- pushing toy cars along a road (a chalk line drawn on the ground outside or a play mat with roads printed on it)
- using a stapler
- making and flying kites
- building an icy pole tower with glue
- counting and stacking coins with left or right hand
- playing a blindfold game: identifying objects by touch
- making or copying patterns in a tray of sand, dirt, shaving cream or flour
- making a collage using pieces of paper, egg shells, buttons, bark and fabric
- making pipe-cleaner animals
- making paper balls: glue strips of paper into a ball shape
- playing with magnets to pick up pins, nails or paperclips
- making paper chains
- doing household jobs, such as washing and drying dishes, setting the table, dusting, sorting and cleaning cutlery, or washing dishes (preferably plastic and not likely to break!)
- transferring pegs from a row on a pegboard into a container, first just with fingers and then with tweezers or tongs
- throwing and catching quoits, beanbags or soft balls
- tying different 'knots' using string and rope of varying thickness.

Use the list above to check your child's fine motor skills and to keep them interested in fine motor activities. Doing a variety of these every week will help continue their development.

## Play-dough recipe

Mix half a cup salt, 1 cup flour, 2 tablespoons cream of tartar.

Add 1 cup water, 1 tablespoon oil and half a bottle of food colouring.

Stir over medium heat for 3–5 minutes, until dough is pliable.

Store in a freezer bag in a sealed container.

# 5  Learning styles

*Each and every person has their own particular style. We each have very different likes and dislikes. The same is true for the way we like to learn.*

## Visual learners

Some people prefer to have the information presented in a visual way. The information can be presented in written material in books, on posters or on a blackboard.

These learners take information from:

- maps
- pictures
- posters
- information sheets
- video and television.

## Auditory learners

Others prefer to learn in an auditory way—the information is told to them. They learn best from hearing the information, or by associating it with sounds and rhythm. These people often have a strong 'musical' interest also.

Auditory learners prefer to learn the information from:

- songs
- speaking

- chants
- rhymes
- radio programs
- music
- rhythmic ways.

# Kinaesthetic learners

Still others need kinaesthetic information to learn. They need to 'do' the task to learn it, to physically act it out by moving around the room and placing their body in particular ways. This style of learning involves processing the particular position of the body, or the way the body needs to move in order to succeed.

These learners prefer to:

- act out the information, story or problem
- learn by doing the activity
- hold things
- feel things
- touch things
- taste things.

# Covering all the bases

Most people will be strong in one style of learning. They might learn best from visual information but if the material is presented in an auditory way that does not mean they will not learn anything. It only means that they might have found it easier and quicker to learn from a map than from hearing about India.

When teaching a new skill to anyone it is best to cover all bases. Try to make sure you present the new information in a visual way and an auditory way, as well as allowing the person to practise 'doing' the new information. One activity from each of the learning styles above will help your child learn the new skill.

In this way, you will ensure your child has been exposed to the information in their best mode, as well as having had access in the other learning styles to support and add to the information already obtained.

Don't punish yourself with too many expectations though. Do what is comfortable and fun for you and your child. The lists are there to help you with suggestions and ideas, not to make you feel inadequate or unprepared. Use them to guide you, not to discourage you from having a go!

## At school

Most education is focused in the visual and auditory areas of learning. Teachers do build in some kinaesthetic experiences for the children, but with so much material to get through every day, and so many children to teach all at once, it is not always the most practical method of getting the material to the children, especially after the first three years of school.

## At home

Obviously, it is important that children be given the opportunity to combine all these styles to ensure they learn the things we are trying to teach them. It's important that they have access to visual, auditory and kinaesthetic information about what they are learning.

- Present the information in a visual way on flash cards, charts and in writing.
- Talk, sing, dance and play with the information.
- 'Do' the information (e.g. place your bodies in the shape of an 'A').
- March to songs about the information.
- Make up chants about the information.
- Lay out sticks in the shape of the letter or word.
- Write in sand.
- Use mud, play dough, magnetic letters and numbers.

- Provide a lot of different textures and experiences of the learning.
- Use colours and tastes to add to the experience.
- Remember to play at everything your child is learning. It will help them to remember what they have learnt.

## Checklist for learning styles*

| Your child's learning style | Yes/No |
|---|---|
| 1 (a) Does your child like maps? | |
| (b) Does your child enjoy picture books? | |
| (c) Does your child watch others and mimic them? | |
| (d) Does your child enjoy computer games? | |
| (e) Does your child like to draw and copy others' pictures? | |
| 2 (a) Does your child enjoy music? | |
| (b) Does your child learn the words of songs easily? | |
| (c) Does your child enjoy rhythmic chants and games? | |
| (d) Can your child mimic you exactly when speaking? | |
| (e) Does your child like to talk about what they are doing? | |
| 3 (a) Does your child show a preference for physical games? | |
| (b) Does your child prefer to move than to sit still? | |
| (c) Does your child want to smell and taste things a lot? | |
| (d) Does your child prefer touching things to just looking? | |
| (e) Does your child like to act out stories they are telling you? | |

*Answers to questions
1 (a)–(e) mostly yes = visual learner
2 (a)–(e) mostly yes = auditory learner
3 (a)–(e) mostly yes = kinaesthetic learner

Be aware that most children under the age of about 4 years would be kinaesthetic learners. The learning in the 0–4 years age group is mostly done through experience. As children become older and more able to think abstractly, they need to 'do' or learn by actually experiencing less and less. They can think through the problem and imagine or suggest answers.

Your child's learning style may still be kinaesthetic but may shift over the next year or so. It could be worth answering these questions again later to check if this has occurred.

This checklist is to be used as a guide only to the ways your child will find learning easiest and most pleasurable. Even if your child appears to be a visual learner according to the checklist, it is important that you expose them to a variety of learning experiences to further enhance their learning.

# 6 Resilience

*The best indicator for success in life is the ability to 'bounce back' after difficulty, and to persist in the face of challenges. People who achieve in life have this ability to work through mistakes, forgive themselves and move on to the next situation. This is a skill we all need, and so does your child. You need to teach that mistakes are not a problem but part of the learning process, and that by making mistakes we learn more. Everybody makes mistakes. Allowing your child to see you make a mistake and then have another go to correct the mistake can help them understand that learning involves mistakes. Mistakes are not impossible to solve, unforgivable or an indication of stupidity as so many people seem to believe, but merely a step in the learning process, usually easily fixed, forgiven or never to be repeated. They are valuable learning experiences.*

The fear of failing will stop people from even trying something new, from having a go. If the fear is large enough, then the person will find a way to not even attempt the task. Sometimes, children learn to be afraid of being wrong, afraid of making mistakes. This fear inhibits their willingness to have a go at new problems or to try to learn a new skill. It can interfere with their learning at school.

By avoiding learning something new, by being afraid even to try, the child can be seen as lacking ability, and this can lead to some children being labelled lazy, slow or low-ability. It is very important that your child know that making mistakes is not something to be afraid of, but normal and a part of the learning process. Remember to reward your child for attempting new things and encourage them to keep trying even when they do make mistakes.

- Encourage your child to see that mistakes are part of the learning process.

- Reward your child for attempting new things.

- Encourage your child to keep trying until they master the new thing.

- Praise and reward your child every time they master something new.

# Abilities for school and beyond

Schools have tended to value abilities in the verbal and language area, and maths and logical thinking are also highly prized. These are the areas that the reports given to parents used to assess and comment on. However, there are many other abilities that are just as worthwhile but that did not always bear commenting on in a school report.

The thinking of educators has changed, and the curriculum is broader to allow other talents and skills to be recognised in the classroom. The child who dances well, is a great athlete, has a musical talent, is artistic and creative, or is good at understanding other people or themselves should also be acknowledged for these abilities.

Good schools and supportive, hardworking teachers recognise and encourage all children to reach their potential in all areas, not just those who show strengths in verbal and language activities, or maths and logical thinking. If you feel your child's talents are not being recognised or valued it may be worth making an appointment to speak to the teacher and/or the principal to discuss your concerns.

Remember to tell your child when you see them doing something well. Encourage, applaud and celebrate all your child's successes. Any talent or ability should be nurtured. Remind your child all the time about what they are good at. It may develop into a career later in life.

- Encourage your child to reach their potential in all areas, and to appreciate all their abilities, talents and skills.

- Allow your child to practise those things they are good at whenever there is an opportunity.

# Some advice before you read on

As with everything, if you are not in the mood, the experience is likely to be far less enjoyable. It's important that you understand that none of the activities suggested from this point on is prescribed. You do not have to do any of them. They are only suggestions and you should pick and choose what you like from them, what works for you and your child.

If you tried to do everything that is suggested here, you would probably burn yourself and your child out. Experiment—try and see—and don't be discouraged too much if the first time you try something it isn't very successful. Leave it and come back to it later—weeks later, if you like. Or leave it out altogether: there is no obligation here.

- Your interest is the first advantage you have already given your child.
- Try and see—if you don't like any activity, leave it out. Do what comes easily and is fun for you and your child, and then build on that success.

# Timing it right

Timing is important too. If you have had a stressful day, then it's probably not the right time for you to be trying something new with your child. Try to choose times when you have plenty of time on your hands, and are in the right (patient) frame of mind for playing around with the suggestions here. Rushing or being frustrated and distracted will interfere with your child's focus and can lead to a negative experience. This may discourage your child next time.

- Create the right atmosphere.
- Provide plenty of stimulation and different opportunities every time.

# Don't push yourself or your child too hard

Give yourself a break, and don't punish yourself too much if you don't have a lot of time for this. Take advantage of the times you do have, any time you put in is worthwhile! Most of all, have fun with your child. At this early stage it should all be fun and exciting. If it's not, then stop and go back to something you did have fun with. Don't leave your child or yourself with a feeling of failure.

The time you put in is worthwhile—even if it's only a little time.

# Breeding success

If you do what you can, when you can, and always give the best of yourself, then you will already be setting your child up for success. It's important that you do what you can to ensure the environment is right, and then encourage, applaud and make sure your child knows how proud you are of them. You know yourself that when you are good at something, it makes you keen to do it again, and practice makes perfect! The more successful your child feels, the more they will want to repeat the experience.

- Success breeds success.
- When your child succeeds, there's already incentive to go on and do more.
- Success is the best motivator in the world!

# 7 Oral language

*Generally, though not always, learning tends to follow the pattern of oral exploration, reading and then writing. They do develop alongside one another, but it's almost impossible to learn to read or write if you don't have oral language first.*

## First things first

You need to be sure that your child is exposed to lots of language. Talking is the first tool your child develops for learning. Being able to hold a conversation, looking at the person you are speaking to, following and understanding the speech of others, following instructions and asking and answering questions are all important skills for your child to master.

If children do not have the language to express themselves then it is very difficult for them to interact with other children, teachers and other parents.

- Talk to your child in clear language.

- Use English if it's not your first language.

- Practise giving instructions and having your child follow them exactly.

- Ask questions and check if your child understands you.

- Expect your child to ask questions when they need information; don't just do things for them.

- Help your child practise speaking clearly so that they can be understood.

- Help your child practise speaking while looking at the person being spoken to.

Encourage your child to speak a lot. Use a lot of different words to say the same things so that they are continually exposed to new words. Talking about words will help stimulate their interest in the variety of words available too.

- Talk about what you are doing and expect your child to do the same.

- Talk about words.

- Practise using different words for the same things.

- Keep a record of all the different words your child knows for the same things.

# Being social

It is very important that your child spends time with other children. This is especially true if your child has not been to preschool, or involved in a crèche or playgroup.

All these places provide opportunities for your child to interact with other children and learn about:

- taking turns in conversation
- expressing needs and wants
- appropriate communication with both adults and children.

It also gives you a sanity break.

There are also other alternatives:

- You may be fortunate enough to have a neighbourhood full of children who you can have over to play and vice versa.
- Your child may show an interest in sporting activities, such as swimming lessons, dancing, football and gymnastics. All can provide opportunities for interaction.

## If your child doesn't talk a lot

Most children love to hear the sound of their own voice, but if your child is very quiet and does not always respond to questions or react to noises, it might be worth having their ears checked.

Very loud children can also have hearing difficulties. A child who always speaks very loudly may be doing so because they have difficulty hearing or can't gauge sound. In this case, it might also be worth having their hearing checked.

Some children are naturally quiet, so it may just be that your child is one who prefers not to talk a lot. It's nothing to panic about, but keep encouraging your child to talk.

Shy children can do just as well at school and tend to be better listeners so they do not miss instructions as frequently as their noisier classmates.

## If your child doesn't hear your instructions

Children may sometimes need to be told something a number of times before they react. There are several possible reasons.

It may be that your child was concentrating on something else and had temporarily filtered out the sound of your voice to help focus. The ability to filter out other noise is a vital one for classroom success, because classrooms tend to be very noisy places at times. So, if your child seems to be able to block out the sound of your voice in order to hear the television, don't despair—they are already developing vital skills for school success!

Before giving instructions it's a good idea to make sure you have the child's attention.

However, if you have made sure the child is focused on you and they still seem unable to follow your instructions, there may be some other problem. A hearing check with your local doctor might be a good idea.

It may also be that your child hasn't developed the ability to remember more than one or two instructions at a time. There may have been too much information. Try giving just one or two instructions at a time, and then increase the number of instructions slowly as your child develops the capacity to remember more. If your child still appears to have a problem following verbal instructions, they may have a sequencing recall difficulty, and a referral to a specialist may assist.

Note, however, that being unable to follow instructions is a different thing from being unwilling to follow them. If a child hears your request and shows this by answering or responding appropriately but refuses to do as they have been told, then this is a different issue altogether and the child may need to be disciplined. How to discipline your child is not part of this book, but it is worth remembering that the consequence of disobedience should be consistent, appropriate and enforced.

## Listening

Listening skills form a vital part of successful communication and are just as important in the classroom as elsewhere in the world.

- Talk to your child.
- Take turns to speak and listen.

- Question your child and listen for appropriate responses.

- Encourage your child to ask questions and listen to answers.

# Children who have problems listening

Children who are unable to listen to others, and who insist on talking over other people, often find school difficult because there is an expectation that the child will listen to others as well as sharing their own ideas and experiences. Basic training in good manners begins here: you speak and I will listen, I speak and you will listen.

Encourage your child to listen by:

- creating opportunities for your child to listen to others

- ignoring any talking that continues while you are speaking

- stopping speaking when your child stops listening.

# Checklist for oral language

| Can your child ... | Yes/No |
|---|---|
| Hear your voice when there is other noise in the room? | |
| Understand your instructions and follow them? | |
| Speak clearly and be understood by others? | |
| Tell you what they want? | |
| Ask questions to obtain information? | |
| Use a variety of words to make themselves understood? | |
| Take turns in conversations? | |
| Listen to what others have to say and respond appropriately? | |
| Talk in appropriate ways to adults? | |
| Talk in appropriate ways to other children? | |
| Play with other children socially? | |
| Understand the speech of others? | |

All learning begins with speaking about it, and from there to reading and writing about it. Being understood is essential for your child's successful involvement in school. If your child has difficulty speaking clearly enough so that they can be understood by others, it may indicate problems with tongue placement or other mouth abnormalities. An assessment by a speech pathologist is recommended if speech problems exist. This assessment should be done early so that the problems can be resolved sooner.

Listening to others forms a central part of successful communication. All children need to learn the skills of listening and responding appropriately to what others say. If your child is having difficulty with this aspect, it is important that you provide opportunities for your child to be social and to talk and listen with others. It may also need further investigation, such as having the child's hearing checked.

# 8 Reading

*It is not essential that your child be able to read a book from beginning to end when they begin school. However, it is important that they be aware that books exist and that there are particular things we do with books.*

- Read with your child: teach your child which way up the book goes.

- Talk about the stories you read. Let your child know how stories go.

- Share your love of reading to inspire your child to read too.

## Reading behaviours

- Let your child see and hear you read regularly. Read for your own pleasure as well as reading to your child.

- If you are not too self-conscious, 'doing the voices' is a great way to get your child involved in the story.

- Show your child how you read. Trace under the words you are reading with your finger. Ensure that your child is aware that reading is done from left to right.

- Make books and reading a part of your daily life. Take time to snuggle on the couch and share a book. Read at bedtime.

- Join the local library and let your child borrow books too. This cuts the cost of reading down considerably, as well as exposing your child to a whole host of people who read.

- Encourage and support any 'reading-like' behaviours your child does on their own (e.g. holding the book and turning the pages, running a finger under the words, making up their own story from the pictures, using book language like 'once upon a time').

- Talk about the book before you start to read it. Look at the cover and try to guess what the story might be about. Talk about the title and how it gives clues to the story.

- Most importantly, talk about the stories you read. Stop in the middle and ask what your child thinks might happen. Help them explain why they think that might happen. The story has all the clues: use the pictures and keep going back to the story. Teach your child to be a thinking reader, to guess ahead: it's the true joy of reading.

- When you finish a story, talk about what the 'best part' was. Ask questions and talk about your own reaction to the story. Tell your child what you found funny, sad, interesting and so on.

If your child is already involved in stories and books then they are ready for the next phase.

## Learning about the sound–symbol relationship

It's not as intellectual as that makes it sound. Learning about the sound–symbol relationship means developing the understanding that each letter in the alphabet stands for a particular set of sounds. For example, the letter 'A' makes a long sound like the name of the letter in the word 'able' and a shorter sound as in the word 'apple'.

When we see the letter 'A' in writing, we understand that it will make one of these sounds in relationship with the other letters. Your child does not need to know all that. (You probably don't want to either!) It's enough that you begin making your child aware that each letter makes a sound.

Most children know the alphabet (they usually can sing it) when they start school. Learning about the letters is the next natural step. Singing the alphabet is good, saying it is also good, and doing either while looking at the alphabet is better.

- Sing the alphabet.

- Say the alphabet while pointing to the letters you are saying.

- Talk about the sounds the letter makes.

- Talk about words with that sound.


## Alphabet charts

You can buy an alphabet chart from the bookshop or toyshop but, better still, why don't you and your child make your own?

- Get some poster paper, fat felt-tipped pens, newspapers, magazines, junk mail.

- Write or cut out each of the sounds.

- Find something that begins with that letter to cut out and paste it on the poster with the letter. Draw it yourself if you can.

- Talk about the sound you are working on and let your child find pictures they want to include that begin with the right sound.

Then, when you sing your alphabet you point or have the child point to the letter as you sing or say it.

## Flash cards

You can also make your own set of flash cards in the same way to help your child learn the letters.

- Play games with sounds.

- Use magnetic letters pulled out of a hat and have your child find things in the house that start with this sound. Just think of things that start with that sound.

- Draw or cut out pictures and have your child find the letter that the object begins with.

- Play Snap, Fish or Memory with letter cards. (You'll need a double set of letters for most games.)

- Play 'I-spy' as your child gets better with the sound (the starting sound of the letters).

Encourage and applaud all your child's efforts. Reward the child with hugs, kisses, stickers or lollies (even though they are bad for teeth, they tend to be a great motivator).

## Moving on to words

As your child gains confidence with letters, you can move on to the 100 most frequently used words. These are the most commonly used words and make up about half of all reading.

Expert or good readers become so familiar with these words that they no longer even need to read them, but skip along to the next word. This is called automaticity, or automatic reading. Seeing the words a lot of times is the key.

Some children will learn these words with only 100 exposures, others will need 300 exposures, while still others may need as many as 600 exposures to learn them. Every child is different and learns at a different pace. Be patient and don't despair if your child seems to take a long time to learn these words.

Warning: Your child does not have to know all these words before beginning school. Applying too much pressure can be a great turn-off for learning! Have fun, and if it isn't fun—stop.

# 100 most frequently used words

| a | I | it | the | and | in |
|---|---|---|---|---|---|
| of | to | be | is | that | was |
| all | but | he | on | they | as |
| for | her | one | we | are | had |
| his | said | with | at | have | up |
| not | so | you | an | by | do |
| go | if | me | my | no | or |
| big | can | did | get | has | who |
| him | new | now | of | fold | our |
| out | see | she | two | your | back |
| been | came | down | from | into | just |
| like | made | much | over | them | this |
| well | went | when | call | come | here |
| make | must | only | some | then | were |
| what | will | which | about | before | could |
| first | little | look | more | other | right |
| their | there | want | where | | |

## Flash cards

Use these 100 words to make up a set of flash cards. (You can buy a set from some bookstores but they are not cheap and you will need two sets if you want to play Fish, Memory or Snap with them.)

You can also buy magnetic sets and use them on an old baking tray, the fridge, filing cabinet or a magnetic whiteboard to help learn the first 100 words.

The instructions for Fish, Memory and Snap are on pages 60–62. You can use any of these simple games for learning sounds, numbers or words.

## Some suggestions for learning the most frequent 100 words

- Talk about the words.

- Practise picking out the word from a set of about five words.

- Talk about how the word looks.

- Remember the focus is being able to recognise the word automatically.

- Stick a word up on the wall, door or fridge using magnets so your child sees it all the time.

- Focus on one or two words at a time—each should have a different starting letter for ease of recognition.

- Cut the word or letters to make up the word from junk mail or magazines and paste them together.

- Keep a scrapbook with a page for each of the words.

- Set targets, make charts and give stickers for the words your child recognises.

- Keep a chart of progress where your child will see it all the time and can show it to guests and others.

- Let your child show off the new knowledge—it's all practice!

- Keep an eye out when you are shopping or travelling in the car for the words on posters, billboards, newspapers or signs.

# Checklist for reading

| Does your child ... | Yes/No |
| --- | --- |
| Listen to stories every day? | |
| Know what a book is and what we use it for? | |
| Know that reading is done from left to right? | |
| Show reading-like behaviours, such as holding the book up the right way, running a finger along under the words, talking about the story? | |
| Share stories from books with you regularly? | |
| See you reading for your own purposes most days? | |
| Use the picture clues to help work out the story? | |
| Recognise that some books have the same beginnings and endings: 'Once upon a time ... they lived happily ever after'? | |
| Recognise the sounds of the alphabet? | |
| Know that each letter makes some sounds? | |
| Know that every word is made up of sounds? | |
| Already recognise some words, like names and favourite toys? | |
| Already recognise some of the most frequent 100 words? | |

If you answered yes to many of the questions above, congratulations! Your child is well on the way to beginning reading. If your child is not doing some of the things above, it may be that they are too young or not ready yet. To get started, look back over this chapter for some ideas, and then extend and build on what your child already knows.

Remember that if you stop having fun with these ideas it may indicate your child is not ready. Stop! Come back to it some time later.

# 9 Writing

*Writing requires a great deal of fine motor control. To begin with, you can expect that your child's writing will be barely legible. Don't expect to be able to read what your child is writing in the first few weeks.*

There are a few steps you can take to make a difference here as well. The first thing for beginning writers has nothing to do with the actual writing. It's important that you establish good posture and pencil grip for the ease of writing.

Sitting at a table or desk (if you have one) is the best place for writing activities to be done, as this is where almost all writing at school will take place.

## Pencil grip

Pencil grip is important. The pencil should rest lightly between the thumb and third finger with the pointer finger almost 'kissing' the thumb and adding directional control.

Children understand pencil grip best with the explanation that the tip of the thumb and pointer are 'kissing' and the middle finger has gone and hidden behind the pencil because he is embarrassed!

The fingers should be placed fairly close to the pencil nib—a few centimetres away, as this gives the best control

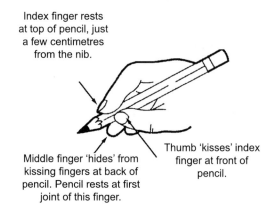

Index finger rests at top of pencil, just a few centimetres from the nib.

Middle finger 'hides' from kissing fingers at back of pencil. Pencil rests at first joint of this finger.

Thumb 'kisses' index finger at front of pencil.

for young hands. Pressure should be light. Pressing the pencil through the paper is fairly common, but this needs to be discouraged. The line doesn't need to go through to the table to be seen.

## Posture

It's important that your child sit correctly while learning to write. The feet should be placed flat on the floor, so your child should sit at a table or desk that is the right height. The chair should be pushed in but the child's stomach should not touch the table edge.

Discourage your child from lying on the table to one side of the writing. Encourage them to sit up fairly straight, with their nose not too close to the paper.

Back should be straight and the face not too close to the paper.

Stomach should not touch the table or desk, but chair should be tucked in.

Height of chair should allow your child to place feet flat on the floor.

- Have your child practise the correct posture when writing.
- Regular practice is important. Practice makes perfect.

If your child seems to need to get very close to the paper when they are writing, it might suggest a visual problem. You should have their eyes checked.

# Paper

It is a good idea to begin using the same paper, and writing in the same way, as your child will be doing at school. It saves some confusion. Many schools use dotted thirds paper, which comes either in books or as loose paper. Dotted thirds have three lines: the base line is a full-line, while the two above it are dotted.

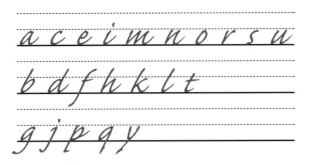

Children write in these dotted thirds using the full line as the bottom of most letters. The middle dotted line forms the top edge of non-capitals such as 'a', 'c' and 'u', while the top dotted line forms the top of any letters with a stick, such as 'b', 'd' and 't'. Letters with a tail, like 'j', 'p' and 'y', begin at the middle dotted line and pass through the base line and down to the top dotted third of the next line.

In schools that don't use dotted thirds, ordinary lined paper is used. Two lines are used for each line of writing, with one left between. The three lines are used in much the same way as the dotted lines.

# Writing is patterns

Writing is mostly about patterns. Letters are all formed from basic patterns, and we place a certain value on these patterns to represent certain sounds.

Horizontal lines, vertical lines, diagonal lines, cups, humps, circles, semi-circles, all form part of letters. They are a great place to start. You can draw the pattern and have your child trace over it, trying not to go 'out of the lines'.

- Start with patterns on blank paper.
- Draw the pattern and let your child trace over it.
- Draw large patterns to begin with, as these are easier while your child develops better control.
- Draw smaller patterns as your child becomes better at tracing.
- Dotted patterns that your child traces over come next.
- Then, draw the pattern and ask your child to copy it, not to trace it.

Dotted pattern

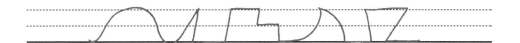

Pattern for tracing over

Child copies the pattern you have drawn

On the dotted thirds paper, have your child draw lines:

- reaching from the top dotted third to the base line (vertical and diagonal lines)
- reaching from the middle dotted third to the base line (humps, cups, semicircles and circles)
- then gradually begin combining shorter sticks with humps to make 'n' and 'm'.

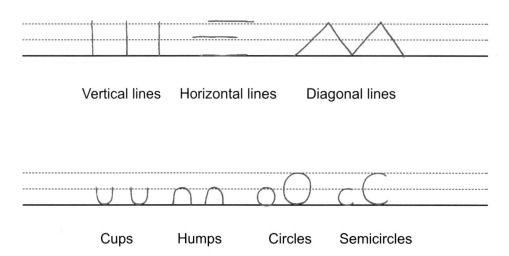

Vertical lines    Horizontal lines    Diagonal lines

Cups        Humps        Circles    Semicircles

Remember to be excited at your child's achievements. Clap, hug, reward, give stickers, tick the work and tell your child how proud you are. Encouragement is the best motivator.

You can use the same method you used to teach patterns to begin teaching your child to write words.

Use meaningful words for your child to write—it ensures interest: your child's name; words such as 'mum', 'dad', 'nanny', 'granddad'; friend's names; pet's names; names of family members; and any favourite story names, are all good beginnings.

## Handwriting books

There are handwriting books available from good bookshops but wait until your child is drawing patterns well before beginning to use these books.

Wipe-clean books with dotted thirds can be found in many good book-stores as well. These are great because you can use them again and again, and also for any younger children.

Warning: Children will usually not be accurate for quite a long time. Going 'out of the lines' is normal. It takes a great deal of practice to be able to trace over patterns accurately, and then to be able to copy accurately. Encourage all attempts and be proud of how your child's writing develops. This is a long and slow process.

Practise, practise, practise!

# Checklist for writing

| Does your child ... | Yes/No |
| --- | --- |
| Sit at a table or desk to perform any writing task? | |
| Hold a pencil with the correct 'kissing method' grip? | |
| Write without pressing the pencil through the paper? | |
| Sit with good posture—without lying on the table or putting their nose on the end of the pencil? | |
| Trace over the patterns you draw without going 'out of the lines' too much? | |
| Trace over larger dotted patterns? (Remember it takes a long time to be able to do this accurately.) | |
| Copy patterns you have drawn accurately? | |
| Have enough control of the pencil to draw straight lines? | |
| Have enough control of the pencil to draw humps, cups, loops, circles, semicircles (large patterns first)? | |
| Understand that letters are made up of patterns (sticks, humps, circles, cups, semicircles)? | |
| Write their own name so that you can read it? | |
| Write the names of other family members or friends? | |
| Write other words that are important to them? | |
| Know how to write using dotted thirds paper? | |

Questions to which you have answered no suggest some areas where you could continue to develop your child's writing skills. Refer back to the relevant section in this chapter for suggestions on how to continue.

Writing is a complex skill, and it takes a great deal of control to be able to write accurately. Don't be discouraged (or allow your child to be discouraged) if your child's writing is slow to develop. It takes a great deal of practice.

# 10 Mathematics

*Counting begins orally: saying the numbers and remembering their order. Have your child practise counting from 1 to 10 first, and then build to counting all the way up to 100. Make up songs or a tune to count to. There are tapes available from bookshops, music stores or specialist early years shops such as The Early Learning Centre.*

- First count from 1 to 10 out loud.
- Use tunes and rhythmic clapping to help your child remember the numbers in order.
- Next count beyond 10, up to 20.
- Count beyond 20.
- Count using a number chart. Point to the number as you are saying it.

## Counting things

Once children have learnt the sounds, they can move on to the notion of counting objects. When it comes to counting, children must begin with concrete materials. They need to count things first. Most children will be unable to count just in their head at first.

Any household item will do for counting practice:

- buttons
- blocks
- balls
- cutlery

- shoes

- fingers and toes (yours and theirs)

- books on a shelf.

Anything will do, so long as they can see and handle the things they are counting.

Moving the object from one pile (uncounted) to another (counted) helps.

## Other ideas for counting

- An abacus can be bought quite cheaply from discount shops.

- Blocks, Lego and beads can be picked up cheaply at garage sales, jumble sales, or for a little more at retail stores.

- Board games with dice are useful.

- Card games (suited to your child's age group) can be played. They also help to build fine motor skills.

- Packs of cards can be picked up fairly cheaply at discount stores, or even in supermarkets.

# Number charts

When counting is well underway, you can make a number chart or buy one from your newsagent or a good bookstore. Begin by pointing to the number while saying it. Play some games where you challenge your child to point to the number that is '3' and so on. Make flash cards and use them to practise recognition of the symbol and how many of something it stands for.

# Adding and taking away

When your child is a competent counter, you can begin adding up and taking away. Make sure you use objects that your child can hold in their hand and move from one pile to the other in order to make these concepts clear. Larger objects can be used initially and then move to smaller objects, which will assist fine motor control too.

- Write the sum out for your child so that they can see how the things they are doing look when written as a sum (equation). Teach the signs for adding (+) and taking away (–).

- Use the same objects for adding and taking away. Using different objects to add together or take away will cause confusion.

- Use things your child can hold in their hand.

- Use larger objects at first.

- Use smaller objects like counters or marbles when the child is able to add or take away easily.

# More than just numbers

While numbers are important, there are a whole range of other concepts that are part of maths that your child should know something about before going to school. These include space (and I don't mean out there where the stars are, but how things occupy space), 2D and 3D shapes, curved and straight lines, symmetry, describing position, measurement of objects, time and temperature, comparing and estimating mass and volume.

Naturally, not all these concepts will be taught immediately, but your child should know:

- the names of many shapes, such as circles, squares, triangles, diamonds, rectangles, ovals
- left and right, up and down, around and through, above and below
- heavy, heavier, light, lighter, more, less
- hot, hotter, cold, colder
- before, after.

# Dot to dot, colouring books and workbooks

There are some terrific workbooks available in good bookshops.

- Dot to dots are great for counting order, and also motor control in the drawing of lines to join the dots.
- Many colouring books also have counting activities and number recognition information.
- Buy wipe-clean books that allow you to re-use the pages. This can help build confidence as your child remembers and can complete the problems more quickly.

# Beyond school

It is important that you continue to use the knowledge your child has learned at school in your daily life. Incorporate counting and using shapes, time, temperature and direction into things you do with your children at home. Baking a cake includes following directions and using temperature in real ways. Playing a board, card or dice game involves using numbers and counting in meaningful ways. Noticing the shapes in a stained-glass window allows your child to practise recognising shapes in the real world. Talking about before and after, earlier and later helps your child become aware of time and sequences of events.

By reinforcing at home what your child is learning at school, you help them to understand the concepts being taught, as well as that learning is fun and is important.

# Checklist for mathematics

| Can your child ... | Yes/No |
|---|---|
| Count from 1 to 10 accurately? | |
| Count objects up to 10 accurately? | |
| Recognise the numbers from 1 to 10? | |
| Identify a number by itself (not on a number chart)? | |
| Add up two groups of the same objects up to 10 in total? | |
| Add up two groups of the same objects up to 20 in total? | |
| Work out a subtraction (take away –), sum starting with up to 10 objects? | |
| Name the shapes of a circle, triangle, diamond, rectangle, oval, square? | |
| Accurately follow directions, including words like 'left', 'right', 'through', 'around', 'above', 'below'? | |
| Understand concepts such as heavy, light, more, less? | |
| *Count from 1 to 100 accurately? | |
| *Count objects up to 20 accurately? | |
| *Recognise numbers between 1 and 100 (using a number chart)? | |
| Work out a subtraction sum starting with up to 20 objects? | |
| *Recognise the symbols for addition (plus, +) and subtraction (take away, –)? | |

*These items are intended as extension activities and are not essential learning before school begins. Not all children will develop these skills at the same time.

Where you have answered yes to some of the questions above, well done! Your child is already doing a number of things that will help them when school begins. If your child is not yet able to do the things listed in the checklist, refer back to the suggestions in this chapter to continue to develop these skills.

# 11 Computers

*There is no doubt that computers will form a part of your child's future. The information technology (IT) arena is the fastest growing employment sector at present and looks likely to continue to expand into the future.*

In ways we have not begun to think about, your child's future will be bound up in information technology. Therefore, it is important that your child have some idea about how to use a computer.

## All things in moderation

There are some terrific games and teaching tools available and you should encourage your child to use a computer regularly, but not to the exclusion of everything else. Computer keyboards are good for motor control, and many games develop good eye–hand co-ordination through the use of the mouse and reflexive games.

- Use the computer to develop your child's eye–hand control.

- Balance your child's time on the computer with time outside and being social.

- Teach your child specific mouse and keyboard skills.

# Alternatives to owning your own computer

If you do not own a computer, then buddy up with a friend who does. When you are visiting at their place, encourage the children to use the computer, but when they are visiting you then find more outdoor or social activities for the children to engage in.

Using the computer also becomes a social exercise if your child is sharing with other children.

## Libraries and cyber-cafés

Most libraries have computers you can access for computer skills, although many of them may not encourage the use of games.

Another possibility is a cyber-café where you can use the computers for a fee. Again, it may not be possible to use them for games, but you can help your child write emails to friends or family who do own a computer and develop keyboard and mouse skills this way. It will be more time-consuming but it makes the use of a computer meaningful for your child. Imagine the excitement of receiving emails back!

# Some concerns

Startling research indicates that children are losing their ability to read emotional and facial signals from their peers, parents and others because they spend so much time reading computer information, playing hand-held games, video games or just watching television. The ability to interact socially with others is a life-skill essential for a successful future, and one that clearly cannot be learnt from computers, video games and television.

Many children are already beginning to suffer difficulties in the classroom because they do not have the social skills necessary to succeed. It's important that a balance is struck between time on the computer, video games, hand-held electronic games and watching television, and social time with physical play activities.

# 12 Games to play

## Snap

Up to four people can play this game but begin with two people when your child is just learning the game.

You will need two sets of picture cards, number cards or word cards—depending on what your child is learning. For learning the sounds of the alphabet, for example, you would need two cards with words beginning with 'a', preferably with the letter and a picture of something that begins  with that sound. (You may want to use two cards showing the same picture to begin with and then increase the challenge of the game by using two showing different things beginning with 'a', such as an apple and an alligator.)

Begin with a small number of cards and increase the number as your child gains knowledge and confidence.

Shuffle and deal the entire number of cards being used between the players.

Each player holds the cards face down in their hand. To begin with, it may be easier to have the cards in a pile in front of each player as young hands may struggle to hold a large pile of cards.

The first player turns the first card in their hand over and places it face up on the floor or table between the players.

The next player turns a card face up on top of the first card. If the two cards match—are the same number, word or sound—the player to recognise this first and place a hand over the top of the cards shouting 'Snap!' gets to keep all the cards in the pile.

This player begins the next round by turning over the first card in their hand.

The game is won when one player has all the cards.

## Memory

You will need a double set of cards for this game.

Play with a set of five sounds, words, numbers (a total of ten cards) to begin with. Increase the number of cards as players become more confident. Begin with sounds, numbers or words your child already knows and add just one or two new words each time you play.

This game can also be played with up to four players. Begin with just two players while learning.

Shuffle the cards and spread them out face down on the floor or table between the players.

The first player turns over two cards, saying the sound, number or word on the card as they are turned over.

If the cards match, the player keeps them and has another turn.

If they do not match the player turns them face down again and the next player has a turn.

Play continues until all the cards have been turned over.

The winner is the player with the most cards at the end of the game.

# Fish

You will need a double set of cards.

You can play with up to four people but begin with two people while learning the game.

Each player is dealt three cards. The remainder of the deck is placed face down between the players.

If a player has a pair (matching cards) in their hand, the pair is placed face up on the floor or table in front of the player.

The player says the sound, number or word on the pair and collects two new cards from the deck.

When both players have three unmatched cards left in their hands, the first player asks one other player, 'Do you have …?', asking for the match to one card in their hand.

If the other player does not have the card asked for, they respond 'Fish' and the first player takes another card from the deck.

If the player asked has the match, they must give the card to the player requesting it but they do not get to pick up from the deck.

Then the next player asks for a match to their card and collects from the other player or draws from the deck.

If a player runs out of cards, they may collect three new cards from the deck.

Play ends when there are no cards left.

The winner is the person with the most matched cards.

# Treasure hunt

For this game you will need a double set of cards.

This game can be played with up to four players.

Begin with just a few sounds, words or numbers to learn.

One player hides one of each card around the house. You might restrict this to one room to begin with. The other players are in another room where they cannot see what the first player is doing.

When the cards have been hidden, the first player calls the others out.

The matching card to one that has been hidden is given to each player who must say the sound, word or number and then find the matching card and say the sound, word or number.

The player who hid the cards may give clues or tell the searchers if they are hot, warm or cold, while they search.

Game ends when all the cards have been found.

# 13 Further reading

Clutterbuck, P., 2000, *Blake's Word Bank: A Handy Book of Graded Word Lists*, Lower Primary, Peter Clutterbuck and Blake Education, Glebe, NSW.

Engelmann, S., 1983, *Teach Your Child to Read in 100 Easy Lessons*, Fireside, New York.

Learning Centre Series, 1997, *How to Manage Learning Centres in the Classroom*, Hawker Brownlow Education, Australia.

McGrath, H., and Francey, S., 1991, *Friendly Kids Friendly Classrooms: Teaching Social Skills and Confidence in the Classroom*, Pearson Education Australia Pty Ltd, South Melbourne.

McGrath, H., and Noble, T., 1995, *Seven Ways at Once Classroom Strategies Based on the Seven Intelligences*, Pearson Education Australia Pty Ltd, South Melbourne.

Parker, A., McSeveny, A., and Sheehan, D., 2000, *Victorian Signpost Maths*, Pascal Press, Glebe, NSW.